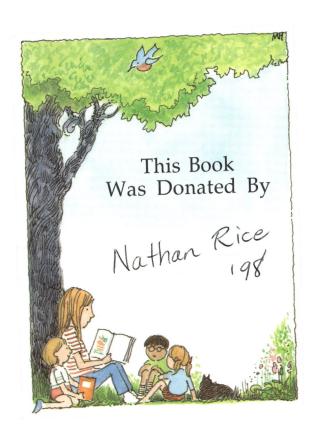

This Book Was Donated By

Nathan Rice
198

Croft Library
Resurrection Christian School

MAPWORLDS
FOOD

©1996 Franklin Watts

First American Edition 1996 by
Franklin Watts
Sherman Turnpike
Danbury, CT 06816

Library of Congress Cataloging in Publication Data

Perham, Molly
    Food / Molly Perham and Julian Rowe.
      p. cm.—(MapWorlds)
    Includes index.
    ISBN 0-531-143740
     1. Food—Juvenile literature. 2. Food crops—juvenile literature.
    3. Food habits—Juvenile literature. [1. Food] I. Rowe, Julian.
    II. Title. III. Series.
    TX355.P37   1995   94-39692
    641.3—dc20   CIP AC

Editorial planning: Serpentine Editorial
Design and typesetting: R & B Creative Services Ltd
Color origination: R & B Creative Services Ltd
Illustrations: Sallie Alane Reason

10 9 8 7 6 5 4 3 2 1
Printed in Great Britain

MAPWORLDS
FOOD

Molly Perham
and Julian Rowe

Illustrated by Sallie Alane Reason

FRANKLIN WATTS
A Division of Grolier Publishing
LONDON • NEW YORK • HONG KONG • SYDNEY
DANBURY, CONNECTICUT

CONTENTS

INTRODUCTION 6-7

CANADA AND THE UNITED STATES 8-9

MEXICO, CENTRAL AMERICA, AND THE CARIBBEAN ISLANDS 10-11

SOUTH AMERICA 12-13

NORTHERN EUROPE 14-15

SOUTHERN EUROPE 16-17

AFRICA 18-19

RUSSIA AND THE FORMER SOVIET STATES 20-21

THE MIDDLE EAST 22-23

SOUTH AND SOUTHEAST ASIA 24-25

CHINA, JAPAN, AND THE PACIFIC ISLANDS 26-27

AUSTRALASIA 28-29

ENOUGH TO EAT 30-31

INDEX 32

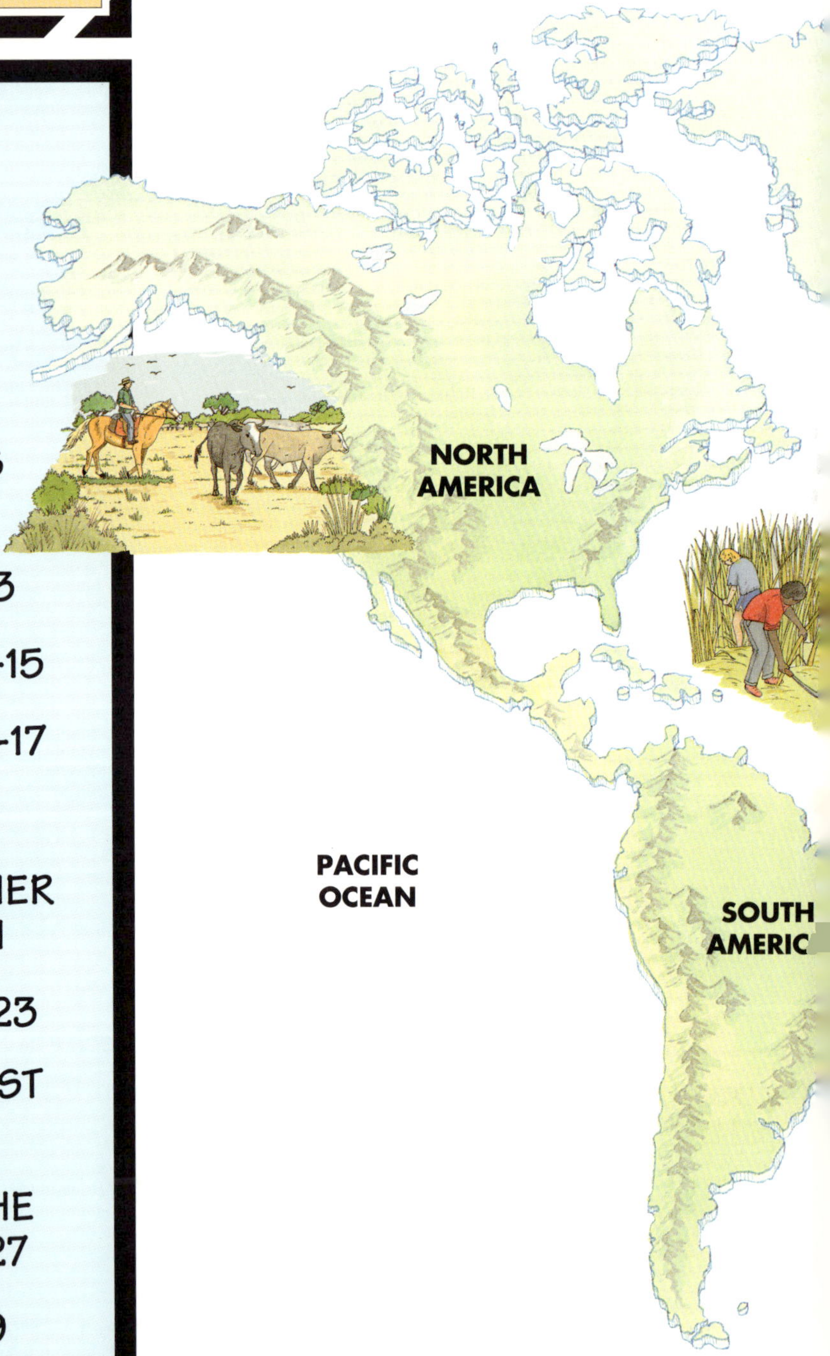

NORTH AMERICA

PACIFIC OCEAN

SOUTH AMERIC

INTRODUCTION

TODAY, OVER HALF the people working in the world either grow, process, transport, or distribute food. Most of the food we eat is prepared from wheat, corn, or rice. These plants are known as cereals, and they are a staple, or main, human food. Another staple food is the potato. Meat, fish, milk, butter, cheese, and eggs are also very important foods.

Food is not shared evenly throughout the world. Some countries can produce more basic foods than their own populations need, while in others people do not have enough to eat. Look at the maps in this book to see the different types of food people farm and eat and where in the world they are found.

An international shopping basket
Where does the food in your shopping basket come from? More than likely, it comes from all over the world. The types of food a country produces depend on its landscape and climate. Modern methods of keeping food and transporting it mean that fresh produce from one country can be delivered quickly to another country thousands of miles away.

- As a globe shows, the earth is round. A map is a drawing of the earth's surface on a flat piece of paper. On each page of this book, an arrow shows which part of the globe is drawn flat on the map.

- A compass tells you which direction is north, south, east, and west. There is a compass like this one at the top of each map.

- At the bottom of each map there is a scale. The scale allows you to work out how far the real distance is between places on the map.

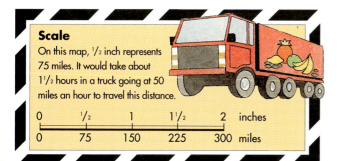

Scale
On this map, ½ inch represents 75 miles. It would take about 1½ hours in a truck going at 50 miles an hour to travel this distance.

| 0 | ½ | 1 | 1½ | 2 | inches |
| 0 | 75 | 150 | 225 | 300 | miles |

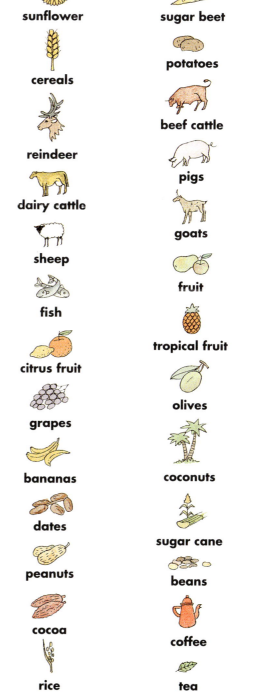

Map symbols:
These picture symbols on the maps show animals and crops in selected places around the world.

sunflower — sugar beet
cereals — potatoes
reindeer — beef cattle
dairy cattle — pigs
sheep — goats
fish — fruit
citrus fruit — tropical fruit
grapes — olives
bananas — coconuts
dates — sugar cane
peanuts — beans
cocoa — coffee
rice — tea

CANADA AND THE UNITED STATES

NORTH AMERICA CONTAINS some of the richest farmland in the world. It can produce more than enough food to supply its own people and so exports large quantities to other countries.

In Canada, to the west of the Great Lakes, the prairies stretch for 1,050 miles. Some of this area is grassland, where millions of cattle and pigs are raised, but much of it is used to grow wheat. The sea off eastern Canada is good for fishing.

The United States produces a lot of oats, rice, corn, rye, barley, wheat, soy, and other beans. Along the Atlantic coast a large variety of vegetables and fruit are grown. The weather in Florida is good for growing citrus fruit such as oranges and grapefruit. There are rich fishing grounds off both the Pacific and Atlantic coasts.

▷ **Fish** is traditionally a staple food of the Inuit who live in Alaska and the far north of Canada. In the past, when the sea was frozen, they cut holes in the ice and lowered fishing lines into the water.

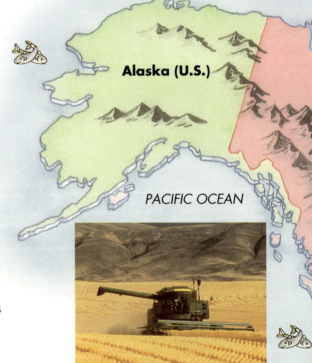

△ **Wheat** is a major crop in North America. New types of wheat are being grown that can resist plant diseases and insect pests. Huge combine harvesters can cut enough wheat in an hour to feed a family for forty years.

▽ **Fast food** started in North America and is now available all over the world. Americans enjoy eating in fast-food restaurants, which serve anything from hamburgers, hot dogs, fried chicken, Mexican dishes, and pizzas, to ice cream and doughnuts.

Scale
On this map, 1/2 inch represents 275 miles. It would take about 5 1/2 hours in a truck going at 50 miles an hour to travel this distance.

0	1/2	1	1 1/2	2	inches
0	275	550	825	1100	miles

MEXICO, CENTRAL AMERICA, AND THE CARIBBEAN ISLANDS

SUGAR, BANANAS, AND COFFEE are the most important crops grown on the tropical islands of the Caribbean. Many people work on the large plantations and in the sugar factories. There is not much pastureland for cattle to graze, so pigs, which need less pasture, are easier to rear. There are lots of fish, and Cuba in particular has a large fishing fleet.

In the north of Mexico wheat is grown and cattle are raised. Maize, or Indian corn, which originated in Mexico, is the main food crop. South Mexico and the other countries of Central America have a tropical climate, which is suitable for growing bananas, pineapples, avocados, and sugarcane.

▷ **Banana** plants grow as tall as trees, but they are not really trees at all, as the "trunk" is made up of leaf stalks. The fruit grows in a large bunch of up to 150 bananas. Each banana is known as a finger, and a cluster of 10 to 12 fingers is called a hand. Bananas are harvested while they are still green. They ripen to yellow on their journey to other countries.

◁ **Tropical fruits** include pawpaws, pineapples, mangoes, avocados, guavas, and coconuts. Breadfruit, cassava, plantains, okra, yams, and akee are popular vegetables.

▽ **Sugarcane** is planted where there is plenty of flat land. The cane reaches up to 20 feet high. At the sugar mill the canes are crushed between heavy rollers to remove the sweet juice from which sugar is made.

◁ **Fish** are plentiful in the warm Caribbean Sea. People catch fish for their own food, or to sell at the local market.

Scale
On this map, 1/2 inch represents 175 miles. It would take about 3 1/2 hours in a truck going at 50 miles an hour to travel this distance.

South America

MANY OF THE WORLD'S FOOD CROPS originally came from South America. The Spanish took potatoes back to Europe in the sixteenth century. The tomato plant, which grew in the Andes mountain region, was taken first to Italy and then to most parts of the world. Other foods that originated in South America are peppers, cassava, and pumpkins. In reverse, settlers introduced into South America sugarcane, coffee, bananas, wheat, rice, and farm animals. Now huge areas of grasslands, or pampas, are devoted to cattle ranching. Maize is the most important staple food in South America and was brought from Mexico by the Incas.

The main exports are beef and coffee. Brazil produces more coffee than any other country in the world, and it is also grown on the hill slopes of Colombia. The coastal waters of Chile and Peru are very rich in fish.

△ **Open-air markets** attract people from the widely scattered villages of Peru. They come to buy and sell such staple foods as maize, beans, fruit, and vegetables.

◁ **Beef** from Argentina, Uruguay, and Brazil is exported all over the world. Cattle are reared on the Pampas grasslands, where they are tended by cowboys known as gauchos.

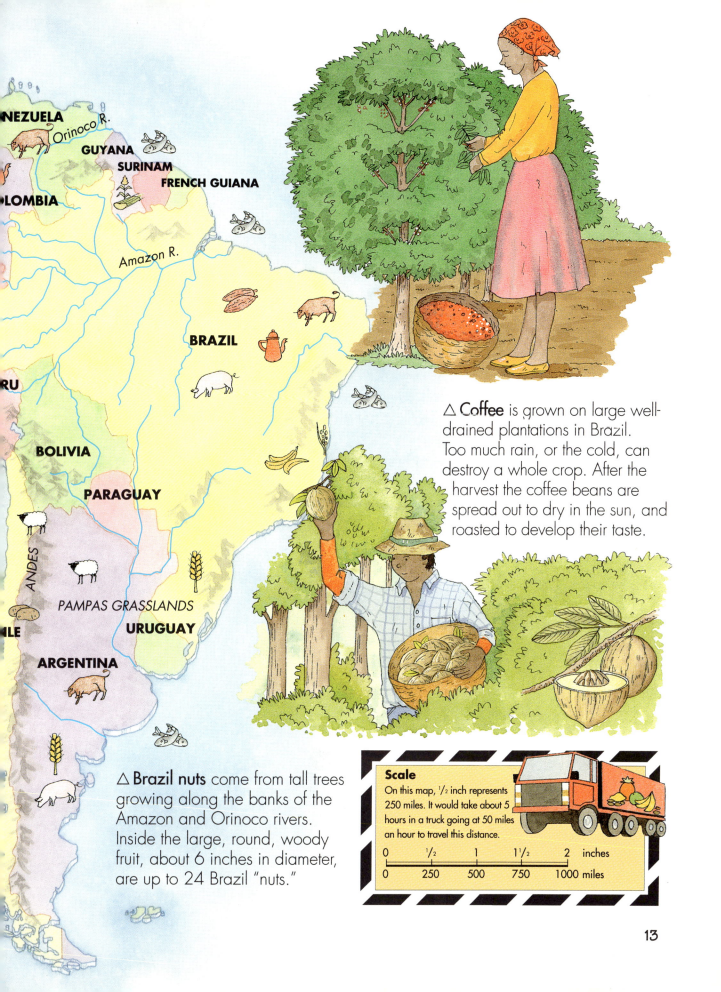

△ **Coffee** is grown on large well-drained plantations in Brazil. Too much rain, or the cold, can destroy a whole crop. After the harvest the coffee beans are spread out to dry in the sun, and roasted to develop their taste.

△ **Brazil nuts** come from tall trees growing along the banks of the Amazon and Orinoco rivers. Inside the large, round, woody fruit, about 6 inches in diameter, are up to 24 Brazil "nuts."

Scale
On this map, 1/2 inch represents 250 miles. It would take about 5 hours in a truck going at 50 miles an hour to travel this distance.

Northern Europe

In NORTHERN EUROPE the main crops are grain, sugar beet, and potatoes. Good grazing land in the west, which is wet, provides rich pasture for dairy cattle. Fishing, especially in Scandinavia where there is little farmland, has always been important. Now fish are also produced on fish farms.

Germany is well known for many different kinds of sausage and a great variety of bread. In Sweden a traditional meal called smorgasbord consists of open sandwiches made with different meats, fish, cheese, and salad. Chocolate cake and whipped cream is a speciality of Austria, and fondue comes from Switzerland. Traditional British food includes roast beef, and fish and chips, and the French are known for their enjoyment of good cooking in general.

▷ **French bread** is bought fresh each day from the baker, *le boulanger*, in villages, towns, and cities all over France. It is eaten with almost every meal.

▷ **Vines** have been grown in Alsace, France, for many centuries. The sunny hillsides have an ideal soil and climate for the grapes used to make the region's famous white wines.

◁ **Most fish** are caught near the coast because the best feeding grounds for fish are found in the shallow water of the continental shelves. Here the great ocean currents, rising from the depths, continually supply fresh nutrients.

▽ **Dutch cheeses** include the round, yellow Gouda, and Edam with its red wax coat. They are made from the milk of cows that graze on the rich farmland of the polders (land reclaimed from the sea and rivers). Many other European countries also produce famous cheeses.

Scale
On this map, 1/2 inch represents 100 miles. It would take about 2 hours in a truck going at 50 miles an hour to travel this distance.

0	1/2	1	1 1/2	2	inches
0	100	200	300	400	miles

SOUTHERN EUROPE

MOST OF THE COUNTRIES around the Mediterranean Sea have warm summers and mild winters. Their climate is ideal for growing many kinds of vegetables and a great variety of fruit, especially citrus. Oranges, introduced into Spain from North Africa, are now an important crop in the area around Seville. Greece grows many lemons and exports them to other countries. Grapes are grown throughout Southern Europe, and each region produces its own type of wine. On stony hill slopes olive trees grow, and sheep and goats browse on the shrubs and grasses. The sea provides fish, shellfish, octopus, and squid.

Mediterranean dishes include pasta and pizzas from Italy, and Spanish paella, a rice dish with chicken and seafood. Greek moussaka is made with lamb and eggplant.

◁ **Celery** is a relatively new crop in this region. It is one of many vegetables grown for export. Fresh produce is packed into crates and flown to other countries.

▷ **Tuna**, or tunny fish, live in the Mediterranean Sea and South Atlantic Ocean. They are caught using nets or, for sport, on a rod and line.

◁ **Pasta** is often made from durum wheat, an important crop in northern Italy. The flour is mixed with water and eggs or olive oil to make a stiff dough, and made into different shapes.

▽ **The olive** has been grown in Mediterranean countries for thousands of years. It is one of the oldest crops in the world. The trees grow slowly and may live for one thousand years.

Scale
On this map, 1/2 inch represents 100 miles. It would take about 2 hours in a truck going at 50 miles an hour to travel this distance.

| 0 | 1/2 | 1 | 1 1/2 | 2 | inches |
| 0 | 100 | 200 | 300 | 400 | miles |

AFRICA

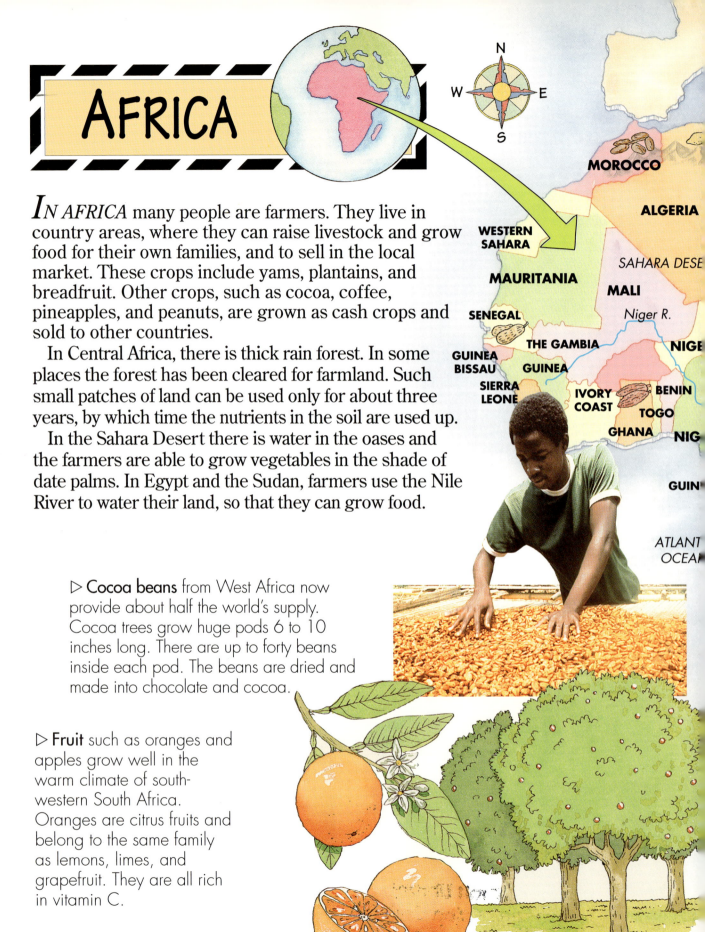

IN AFRICA many people are farmers. They live in country areas, where they can raise livestock and grow food for their own families, and to sell in the local market. These crops include yams, plantains, and breadfruit. Other crops, such as cocoa, coffee, pineapples, and peanuts, are grown as cash crops and sold to other countries.

In Central Africa, there is thick rain forest. In some places the forest has been cleared for farmland. Such small patches of land can be used only for about three years, by which time the nutrients in the soil are used up.

In the Sahara Desert there is water in the oases and the farmers are able to grow vegetables in the shade of date palms. In Egypt and the Sudan, farmers use the Nile River to water their land, so that they can grow food.

▷ **Cocoa beans** from West Africa now provide about half the world's supply. Cocoa trees grow huge pods 6 to 10 inches long. There are up to forty beans inside each pod. The beans are dried and made into chocolate and cocoa.

▷ **Fruit** such as oranges and apples grow well in the warm climate of south-western South Africa. Oranges are citrus fruits and belong to the same family as lemons, limes, and grapefruit. They are all rich in vitamin C.

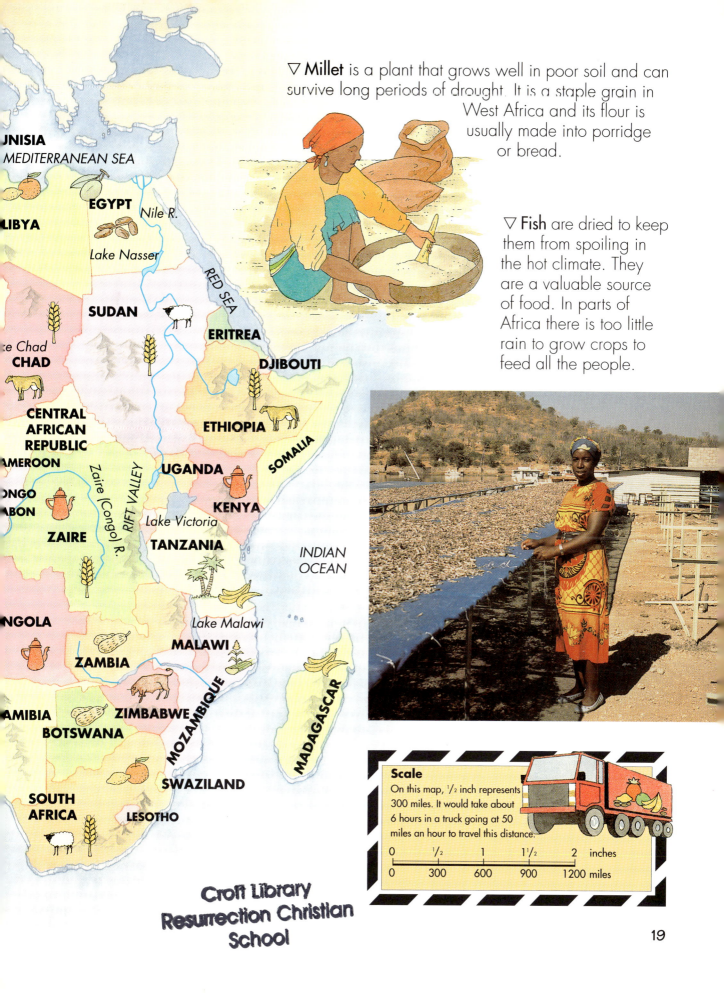

▽ **Millet** is a plant that grows well in poor soil and can survive long periods of drought. It is a staple grain in West Africa and its flour is usually made into porridge or bread.

▽ **Fish** are dried to keep them from spoiling in the hot climate. They are a valuable source of food. In parts of Africa there is too little rain to grow crops to feed all the people.

Scale
On this map, 1/2 inch represents 300 miles. It would take about 6 hours in a truck going at 50 miles an hour to travel this distance.

RUSSIA
AND THE FORMER SOVIET STATES

ONLY A SMALL PART of this huge area can be used for farming. The best farming land is in the west, where most of the people live. The main crops are wheat, rye, barley, potatoes, and sugar beet. Cattle and pigs are reared on the pastureland. Around the Black Sea the climate is mild, and here tea and sunflowers are grown. Fishing is important in the Volga and other rivers, and factory ships travel to the rich North Sea fishing ground.

Central Asia consists mainly of grasslands and sandy deserts. Some of the people there are nomads, who move around from place to place herding sheep and goats. In the southeast the land is barren, and the villagers of the Pamir mountains breed yaks.

△ **Teatime** for a typical Russian family consists of cold meats or pickled herring with bread, sweet pastries, and cakes. Water for the tea is boiled in a samovar.

▷ **Sunflowers** grow well in the warm climate of the Black Sea. Margarine and oil are made from the seeds.

20

◁ **Reindeer** provide meat, milk, and other dairy products for the people who live in Siberia. The reindeer, or caribou, is the only deer that has been domesticated. The reindeer are also used for pulling sleighs.

△ **Caviar** is a great delicacy. It is the eggs of the sturgeon, which breeds in the Volga river and the Caspian Sea. There used to be many of these large fish, but the water of the Volga River has become polluted and the sturgeon have also been overfished.

Scale
On this map, 1/2 inch represents 350 miles. It would take about 7 hours in a truck going at 50 miles an hour to travel this distance.

THE MIDDLE EAST

THE MOST FERTILE LANDS of the Middle East lie along the banks of the Tigris and Euphrates rivers. This area, known as the Fertile Crescent, was where farming first developed 6,000 years ago. Farming also flourished along the banks of the Jordan River and on the coasts. The rest of the land is mostly desert. Where the farmers can get water, from rivers or from wells, they grow a variety of crops. Wheat and barley are grown in the damper north, rice and millet in the hot south. Fruit such as oranges, olives, and grapes grow around the Mediterranean, and dates in the oases.

Sheep and goats are raised for meat. Fishers catch sardines, tuna, and other fish in the coastal waters of the Mediterranean, Red Sea, and the Persian Gulf. New watering, or irrigation, projects have been built, and new types of seeds are being tested in an effort to increase crop production.

△ **Wheat** came from the Middle East thousands of years ago and it is still grown there today. It is used to make pita and shami, the most popular breads.

◁ **Bedouin** nomads herd camels, sheep, and goats in the desert. They sleep and eat in traditional black tents.

◁ **Turkish food** includes shish kebab, made from cubes of lamb roasted on a skewer over a charcoal fire, and dolmas, which are vine leaves stuffed with meat or rice. A meal often ends with a sweet dessert such as halva or baklava.

▽ **Date palms** have been cultivated in the Middle East since 3000 B.C. The tree can live on less water than any other fruit-growing plant. Dates are a staple food and especially popular with people living in desert areas. They are called the "bread of the desert."

Scale
On this map, 1/2 inch represents 110 miles. It would take about 2 hours in a truck going at 50 miles an hour to travel this distance.

SOUTH AND SOUTHEAST ASIA

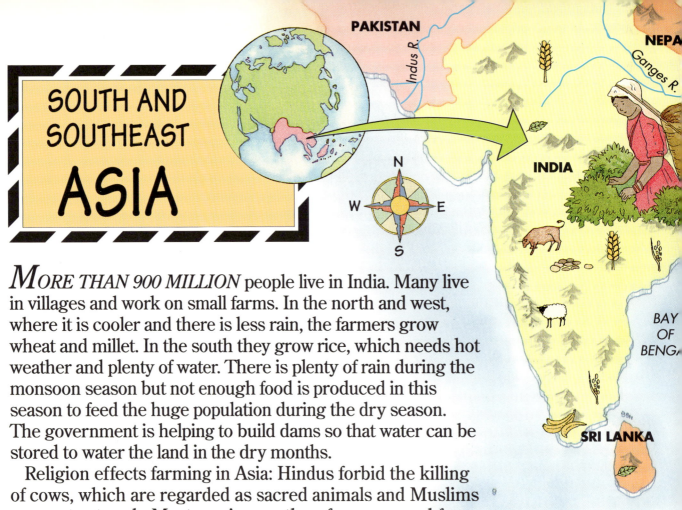

MORE THAN 900 MILLION people live in India. Many live in villages and work on small farms. In the north and west, where it is cooler and there is less rain, the farmers grow wheat and millet. In the south they grow rice, which needs hot weather and plenty of water. There is plenty of rain during the monsoon season but not enough food is produced in this season to feed the huge population during the dry season. The government is helping to build dams so that water can be stored to water the land in the dry months.

Religion effects farming in Asia: Hindus forbid the killing of cows, which are regarded as sacred animals and Muslims may not eat pork. Meat curries are therefore prepared from mutton or poultry.

In Indonesia, large plantations of coffee, tea, and sugar grow on land cleared from tropical forests.

◁ **Spices** are an essential ingredient of Asian cooking. Freshly ground spices are bought from a spice seller, and cooks make up their own special blend for each dish. Red chili powder, yellow turmeric, and ginger are the most popular spices.

◁ **Tea** grows as an evergreen tropical bush. Picking is still usually done by hand. The leaves are dried and crushed before being packed.

▽ **Floating markets** in Thailand take place at the mouth of the Chao Phraya River where it is crisscrossed with small rivers and canals that take water to the fields.

▽ **The Spice Islands** are very hot and wet, and covered in fertile volcanic soil. Nutmeg, cloves, mace, cinnamon, and pepper are traditional crops. Centuries ago Arab merchants would take these spices to Europe.

Scale
On this map, ½ inch represents 150 miles. It would take about 3 hours in a truck going at 50 miles an hour to travel this distance.

| 0 | ½ | 1 | 1½ | 2 | inches |
| 0 | 150 | 300 | 450 | 600 | miles |

CHINA, JAPAN, AND THE PACIFIC ISLANDS

CHINA FEEDS ITS ENTIRE population of more than one billion people – 22 percent of the world's population – by farming less than 7 percent of the world's total farmland. In the south and east of the country, the fertile fields give three harvests each year.

The main islands of Japan are mountainous, and flat areas are few. Hillsides are cut into steps, or terraced, to create flat fields for growing rice and other crops. Rice is the staple food crop. There are rich fishing grounds around Japan and it is famous for its raw fish dishes called sushi.

Sugarcane and pineapples are cultivated in the Philippines.

▷ **Chinese meals** are eaten with chopsticks. Rice, noodles, soy beans, fish, and vegetables are used in Chinese cooking.

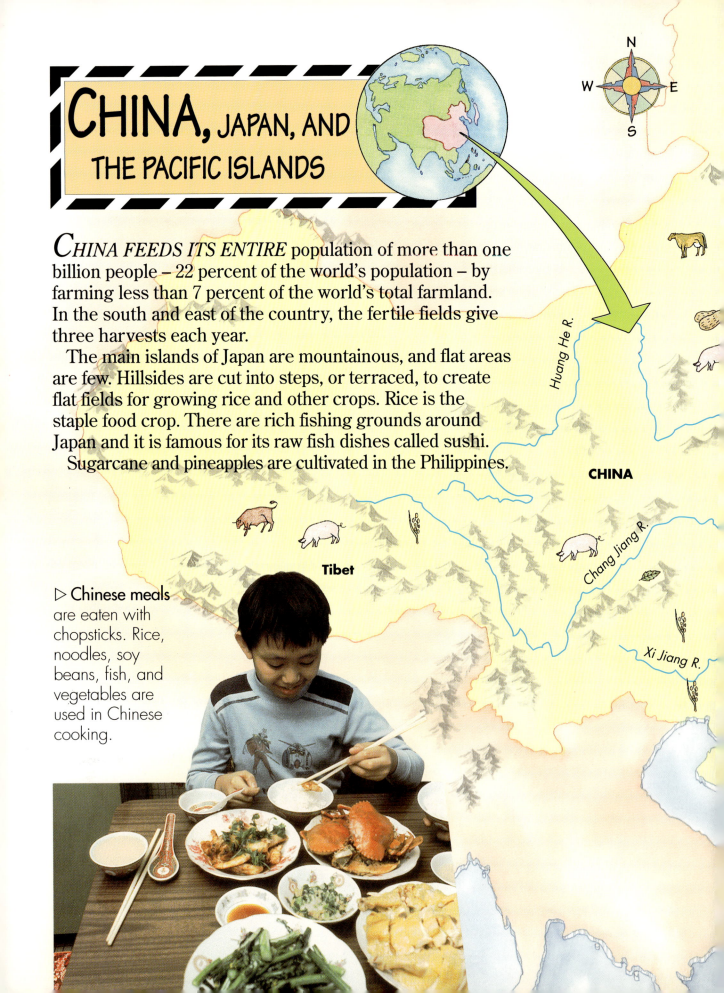

◁ **Soy beans** are one of the main sources of protein for people living in the Far East. They were first grown in China more than 4,000 years ago. Now more than three-quarters of the world's crop is grown in North and South America.

◁ **Rice** is the staple food in the south and east regions of China, as well as in most of Asia. Rice is first planted in seed beds and the young seedlings are transferred into flooded paddy fields.

▽ **Coconut palms** grow along the sandy coasts of many Pacific islands. The ripe coconuts are carried by the sea to other shores, where they quickly take root.

Scale
On this map, ½ inch represents 140 miles. It would take almost 3 hours in a truck going at 50 miles an hour to travel this distance.

AUSTRALASIA

THERE IS A FERTILE STRIP of land on the east and southeast coast of Australia, where most people live. Australia has the lowest rainfall of any continent and in the interior, called the outback, the climate is too hot and dry for farming. In Queensland, in the northeast of Australia, it is hot and wet. Farmers grow sugar cane on the low land. In the milder climate of the southeast, fruit such as peaches, apricots, and pears grow well.

New Zealand became rich through sheep farming. It now exports more lamb and dairy produce than any other country. Lamb, butter, and cheese are taken in refrigerated container ships to Europe, the Middle East, Asia, and the United States.

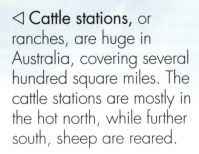

◁ **Cattle stations,** or ranches, are huge in Australia, covering several hundred square miles. The cattle stations are mostly in the hot north, while further south, sheep are reared.

▷ **Fruit** can be grown in the tropics all year round, because the temperature does not change much from one month to the next. In New Zealand, apples, lemons, and kiwifruit are grown and exported to other countries.

PACIFIC OCEAN

◁ **Pineapples** grow on many tropical islands, including Papua New Guinea. Originally from Central America, the fruit is now grown in Asia and in Africa.

PUA NEW GUINEA

EAT BARRIER REEF

CORAL SEA

Queensland

rling R.

▷ **Sheep** were originally bred for their wool and are now also raised for their meat. There are many more sheep in New Zealand than there are people. For every one person there are 16 sheep.

NEW ZEALAND

TASMAN SEA

Scale
On this map, 1/2 inch represents 250 miles. It would take 5 hours in a truck going at 50 miles an hour to travel this distance.

| 0 | 1/2 | 1 | 1 1/2 | 2 inches |
| 0 | 250 | 500 | 750 | 1000 miles |

29

ENOUGH TO EAT

	Key
	Over 2,700 c
	2,200 - 2,700
	Under 2,200
	Figures not available

Although the world's farms produce enough food to feed everybody, the extra food does not always reach the hungry. A vast quantity of food often spoils before it can be eaten, so it is important to find a better way of getting food to people who need it. Because producing meat uses more land than is needed for a vegetarian diet, changing the way land is used could help to provide more food for an increasing world population.

The map on the right shows how much food is eaten around the world. It shows the number of calories, a measure of energy, taken in (on average) by one person each day.

▷ **Different kinds of food**
Wheat, rice, and maize supply nearly half the energy needs of the world's population. These cereals are called carbohydrates. Body-building proteins come from fish, eggs, nuts, dairy products, and meat. Fresh vegetables and fruits are good sources of vitamins and provide fiber. Vitamins are needed in varying amounts to help keep your teeth, skin, and blood healthy.

◁ **Intensive cattle rearing**
Cows are kept in barns or sheds. In very hot countries, this means that they can keep cooler in the shade. Their food, or fodder, is brought to them and this helps to increase the amount of milk they produce.

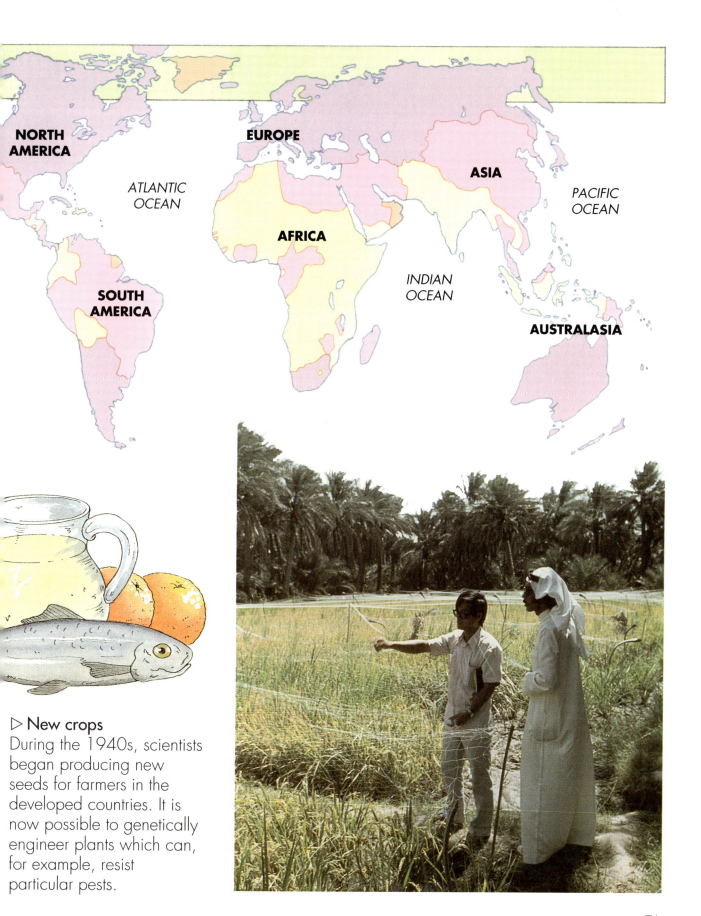

▷ **New crops**
During the 1940s, scientists began producing new seeds for farmers in the developed countries. It is now possible to genetically engineer plants which can, for example, resist particular pests.

Index

apricots 28
avocados 10, 11

bananas 10, 12
barley 8, 20, 22
beef 8, 12
Brazil nuts 13
bread 14, 19, 22
breadfruit 11, 18
butter 6, 28

calories 30
carbohydrates 30
cash crops 18
cassava 11, 12
cattle 8, 10, 12, 14, 28, 30
cattle ranching 8, 12, 28
caviar 21
celery 16
cereals 6
cheese 6, 15, 28
Chinese cooking 26
chocolate 18
citrus fruit 8, 16
climate 6, 8, 14, 16, 28
cocoa 18
coconuts 11, 27
coffee 10, 12, 13, 18, 24
container ships 28
corn 6, 8

dairy produce 14, 21, 28
dates 18, 22, 23
deserts 20, 22, 23
dolmas 23

eggplant 16
eggs 6, 30
energy 30
exports 8, 28

fast food 9
Fertile Crescent 22
fish 6, 8, 10, 12, 14, 15, 16, 19, 20, 26, 30

fish farms 14
fondue 14
fruit 8, 11, 12, 16, 18, 22, 28

goats 16, 20, 22
grapefruit 8, 18
grapes 14, 16, 22
grasslands 8, 12, 20
guavas 11

hamburger 8, 9

Inuit 8
irrigation 22

kiwifruit 28

lamb 28
lemons 16

maize 10, 12, 30
mangoes 11
markets 12, 18, 25
meat 6, 21, 22, 24, 30
millet 19, 24
moussaka 16

new crops 8, 22, 31
noodles 26
nuts 13, 30

oats 8
octopus 16
okra 11
olives 16, 17, 22
oranges 8, 16, 18, 22

paella 16
pasta 16, 17
pawpaws 11
peaches 28
peanuts 18
pears 28
peppers 12
pests 8, 31
pigs 8, 10
pineapples 10, 11, 18, 26, 29
plant diseases 8

plantains 11, 18
potatoes 6, 12, 14, 20
prairies 8
protein 27, 30
pumpkins 12

rainfall 13, 24, 28
reindeer 21
rice 6, 8, 12, 24, 26, 27, 30
rye 8, 20

sausages 14
seeds 22, 31
sheep 16, 20, 22, 28, 29
shish kebabs 23
smorgasbortd 14
soy beans 8, 26, 27
spices 24, 25
staple food 6, 8, 12, 19, 27
sturgeon 21
sugar beet 14, 20
sugarcane 10, 11, 12, 24, 26, 28
sunflowers 20
sushi 26

tea 20, 24, 25
tomatoes 12
transporting food 6, 28
tropical fruit 11, 28
tuna 16

vegetables 8, 12, 16, 26, 30
vines 14
vitamins 18, 30

water 18, 22, 23, 24
wheat 6, 8, 10, 12, 20, 22, 24, 30

yaks 20
yams 11, 18